Broken

Elena Mary Liakata

Broken © 2022 Elena Mary Liakata

All rights reserved.

No part of this publication may be reproduced, stored in a retrieval system, or transmitted, in any form or by any means, electronic, mechanical, photocopying, recording or otherwise, without the prior written permission of the presenters.

Elena Mary Liakata asserts the moral right to be identified as author of this work.

Presentation by *BookLeaf Publishing*

Web: www.bookleafpub.com

E-mail: info@bookleafpub.com

ISBN: 9789357695350

First edition 2022

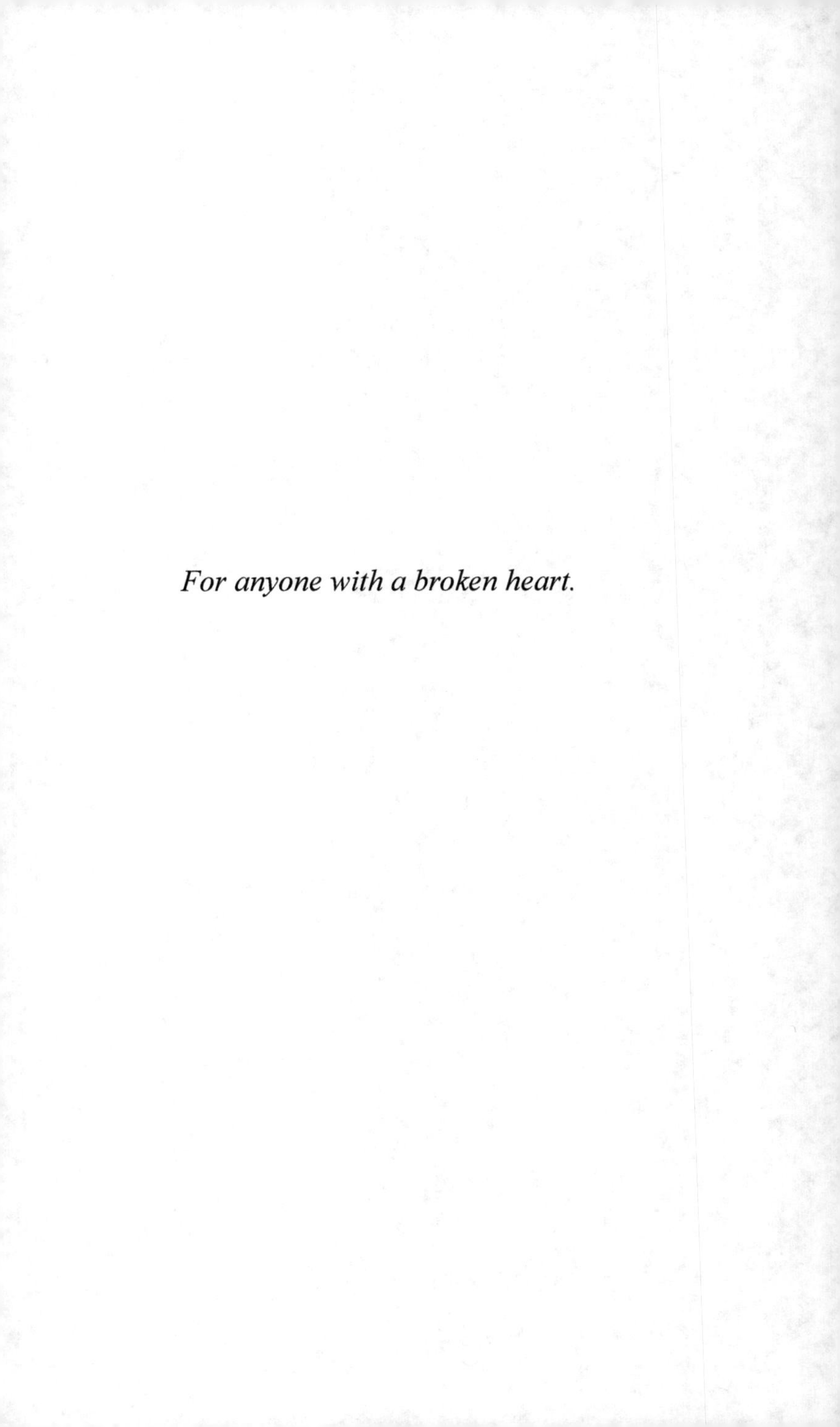

For anyone with a broken heart.

Warning signs

The first time we met I couldn't look into your eyes.
It must be love I thought.
When I first saw you I couldn't find the words to describe how I felt.
It must be real I thought.
The first time we went for a walk my hand was shaking so hard I could not touch you.
This is what it's like, I thought.
What I didn't know was that my body was warning me of what was to come.
My gut was telling me this is not right.
I had never felt this way before so I wanted to believe it was love.
But it was not. It was hurt. It was pain and suffering waiting to happen.
I couldn't look at you because in your eyes I could see my heartbreak.
I couldn't speak because in my thoughts I could hear my cries.
I couldn't move because in my body I could feel the knives that you would put through me.
Always listen to your instincts.

Broken

What hurts the most isn't you leaving,
You didn't break my heart because you decided
not to love me anymore,
because you never did.

Realising you were my whole world and I was a
mere second in your life.
Realising I would do anything to make you
happy but you wouldn't even try.
Realising that you were my one but I was not.

That's what broke my heart.

Confusion

Realising you were never who I thought you
were came as a shock.

You were never kind so why did I see kindness?
You were never sweet so why did I see
sweetness?
You were never caring or giving or helpful so
why did I find all these qualities in you?

The answer is I never did. I was trying to find
the good in you. Trying to see what you could be
if you wanted.

But you never did.

The love of my life

I thought you were the love of my life
But the love of my life won't make me cry on
my birthday
The love of my life won't blame me for the
mistakes people made in your past
She won't hit on other girls in front of me
And she won't push me away when she needs
me the most
The love of my life won't make me question
whether I will ever be good enough
The love of my life won't make me change my
hair
She won't make me feel guilty for living in a
different city
She won't talk to me the way you did
The love of my life will be kind and gentle.
She'll be easy and sweet.

The love of my life is waiting for me .
How wrong I was to think it could be you.

My missing piece

We leave a piece of us with every person we
meet.
We leave a piece of us in every human
interaction we have.
We leave a piece of us everywhere we go.

But I left a big piece of me with you.

I wasn't expecting to have to leave.
You woke me up in the middle of the night and
told me I had to go so I took with me all I could.
My pieces were too heavy to carry.

I was tired. I was scared. I didn't know what to
do. I didn't know where to go.

I thought I could come back and collect it.
I thought you would bring it back to me.
I thought it would be ok.

But it wasn't and I didn't and you didn't.

I left the biggest part of me with you and that
hurt the most.

Maybe it explains why I feel so empty. Because
I'm missing my piece.
The piece I have so desperately tried to take
back the last 3 months.

I don't want it back anymore.

You can keep it.

Maybe you have thrown it away.

Maybe that piece of me is somewhere lost and
long gone.

Maybe I have been looking for something that
can never be found.

Maybe I have been mourning the wrong thing.

I have been mourning you when I should be
mourning me.

I should be mourning my piece. My missing
piece.

I now have to build a new one.

It will be strong, stronger than it was. But I must
be careful not to build it too fast.

I don't want my new piece to be part of you.

I don't want to be bitter.
I don't want to be cruel
I don't want to be selfish
I don't want to be you

I must find me.

I must find me after you
I must build my new piece without you.

Someone else

You have moved on.
You have found someone new to love.
This makes me burn, makes me cry, makes me
dissolve in all my sadness.
It makes me question whether you ever felt
anything for me.

I was never good enough.
I could never change you, you said.
It would never work, it would never be.

You found someone.
You found someone that is not me.

How can that be?

Why

Why do you get to be happy?
Why do you get to smile with her when I am
dying inside.
My heart keeps pouring blood while you look at
her
My wounds keep growing while you kiss her
My scars get deeper while you touch her.

Why is it that you get to come into my life and
cause me so much pain yet you get to move on?

It's not fair.
It's not ok.

Lost and found

Have you ever noticed what the lost and found box looks like?

Full of odd T-shirts and old coats. A single glove and a ripped scarf.

Oh that's odd, there's a sock, I wonder who left it behind.

You can find all sorts in the lost and found box. Things that were once loved.

Once loved but now forgotten.

On the odd occasion people come rummaging through and find something they think is theirs you find a little hope. You found the person you belong to. But very fast you realise, they realise , you're not theirs at all. They were wrong, they changed their mind.

Back into the box.

Lost and found.

I'm lost.

I need to be found.

She

She said she loved the way I looked at the sky.
She said she found it funny how I loved reading
so much yet I would rarely be able to finish a
book.
She said my eyes were the most beautiful she
has ever seen.

Yet she did not love me.

She thought I was kind and had a heart of gold.
She thought she didn't deserve me.

Yet she did not truly want me.

She laughed at my jokes and smiled back at me
every time.

Yet she was never truly mine.

Pain

I don't understand what has happened to me

I'm scared I'm losing my heart
My heart keeps jumping when I think of you and
realises that you've gone.
My heart is scared
It feels like it's stabbed, it's bleeding and I can
feel the blood gushing out of it and it won't stop

it hurts.

This pain is real

I'm my chest

I can feel it

Where do I go?

Where do you go after giving yourself to
someone?
When you have folded you heart and soul into a
neat pile and handed it right over to them.

I have nothing left. I forgot to keep some of
myself for me. I was too busy making sure
everybody had a piece of me, too busy making
sure everyone was happy with me, too busy
trying to care for everyone else that I forgot to
care about me.

What do you do when you feel like you have
nothing left to give? Nothing left to feel ?
Nothing left to say.

I've given all my smiles and reassuring glances
away. I have no helping words left and no more
inspiration.

I feel empty. Like a carton of milk that has been
used up. I've been poured into so many glasses
in hopes that I will be able to support the lips
that so easily soak me up but all that's left is an
empty carton.

What do you do with an empty carton? You put
it in the bin.

There is no more use for me, I've been used up.

But who told you you were supposed to be
everyone else's? What about you?

Love like this

You say I have had my heart broken before
You say I have been through sadness and come
out stronger
You say it will be ok
But it's not.
Never have I loved like I have loved you
Therefore never has the pain been so
excruciating
Never have I kissed like I have kissed you
Therefore the sadness is devouring
Never have I laughed like I have laughed with
you
Therefore the memories are overwhelming
Never have I given like I gave to you
Therefore the emptiness is endless .

You say I need to move on.
You say I need to get over it.

I'm sorry my dear but that's not how my heart
works.

The day you left

17

The day you left me felt like a thousand pieces
of glass cut through my soul
Each sharp piece piercing me deeper and deeper
until it would go no more
The day you left me I died a silent death
I Screamed silent screams
and bled invisible blood.
The day you left me was unlike any other
before.

Drowning

And when you're drowning
Who will save you?
When you've spent your whole life floating
How do you let go of what's pulling you down ?
Save me from my own sorrow
Please

The real you

I feel empty
I feel embarrassed
I feel ashamed

It's a strange kind of feeling to know you have
invested everything in someone who doesn't
really exist.

I can see clearly now.

I can see everything you did, everything you
said and everything you are.

I can't believe I ever saw anything good in you.

I'm so confused. Why could I not see the real
you?

Fuck you

You are not a nice person.

You aren't kind

You never were.

Fuck you for taking advantage of me .

The girl that used to have a heart

I can feel my heart breaking,
I can feel my heart bleeding
I am afraid it's gone for good
I am afraid after this there will be nothing left

A shell of a human who once had a heart

She used to be different they will say
She used to care
Now all she does is spend her day waiting for
nightfall to come

In the night when she's alone in her room
Alone with herself and her thoughts

Because everyone leaves

Everyone
will
leave

I'm sorry
she whispered to her old self
to the girl that used to have a heart

How dare you

How dare you say it was nothing.
How dare you say we weren't together.
How dare you say it was only a few months.
How dare you try and pretend my emotions
aren't real.
How dare you.
How dare you.
How dare you.
HOW DARE YOU.

What it's like

It's like being in a room full of people but no
one can see you
You are screaming at the top of your lungs but
no one can hear you
It's like drowning in a pool filled with people
but no one saves you, because no one knows
you're drowning.

And every time someone reaches out it feels like
a burden. Something I have to do. Add it to the
list of messages I have to reply to.

And even though I know these people love me, I
don't feel the love. I feel numb and alone.

What's the point. I don't know anymore.

I don't enjoy walks . But at least I can still
appreciate a pretty sunset. You haven't taken
that away from me yet.

Letter to myself

To past me

Dear me,

I wish I could give you a hug.
I wish I could wipe your tears away.
I wish I could hold you at night and tell you that
everything will get better
Because it will, eventually.

It will be hard then it be even harder and when
you think you can't take life anymore , when
you reach your absolute low
Then my little girl you will find the strength to
push back.

You will find the strength to stand back up on
your two feet.
You will laugh again
And you will love again
You will feel again

And it will be so good.
The best feeling you've ever had.
It won't take away the pain you once felt

But it will help you look back and remind
yourself to never allow anyone to have a hold on
you like that
No one who does not deserve your love
No one that is not worthy

Cause you, my little girl, you are worthy.

www.ingramcontent.com/pod-product-compliance
Lightning Source LLC
LaVergne TN
LVHW051249200726

843510LV00011B/1765